THE ARAB
AND
HIS RABBI

D1520926

THE ARAB
AND
HIS RABBI

A Story of Awakening

YACOUB GIBRAN

CONTENTS

Introduction

January 2020 felt like the beginning of an extraordinary period in my life.

I was starting a new job as the general manager of one of the most luxurious fitness centers in South Florida. And I had just moved into an oceanfront condo in Bal Harbour.

I had always wanted to live on the beach. To realize that goal, I had worked hard and put in long hours training my clients at the gym, saving all the money I could, and finally I was able to rent a beautiful one-bedroom beachfront condo right on Collins Avenue.

I loved my new home. I was eager to sit on the balcony to enjoy a hot cup of coffee in the morning before going to work, and I looked forward to having my protein shake there in the evenings after finishing my strenuous gym workouts.

I was beyond passionate about working out, and my clients felt my enthusiasm for the fitness lifestyle. They were more than just clients: they were raving fans, and they constantly referred their family members and friends to me. My business was booming.

Little did I know I was about to experience the biggest breakdown of my career as a fitness professional—a breakdown that would ultimately lead to a gigantic, quantum-leap break*through* that would demand a radical departure from my old, habitual patterns. This breakthrough would not have taken place without the mentorship and guidance of my next-door neighbor.

An Auspicious Encounter

I remember well the first time I met Avraham. It was an early morning in January soon after I moved in. I was sitting on my balcony, sipping my double espresso and enjoying the spectacular Florida sunrise.

I heard my next-door neighbor open the sliding glass door leading to his balcony. Our balconies were adjacent to each other, separated only by thin iron railings around their perimeters. As I looked to see who my neighbor was, an older man stepped onto the balcony, smiled, and walked toward me.

I stood to greet him and could not help noticing something magical about the way he carried himself. He was only five foot seven or so, but he seemed much taller. He stood up straight, and his posture was perfect. His eyes were as blue as the clear Florida skies, and they had a glimmer that made him look quite youthful. I could not guess whether he was in his sixties or seventies. I was surprised to learn later that he was in his eighties. I also noticed the yarmulke on his bald head.

He introduced himself as Avraham and told me he had just arrived from New York the night before, adding with a smile that he was a so-called snowbird who spent his winters in Florida. His face was very open and kind; there was nothing contrived about him. He looked me straight in the eye as he spoke, and everything about him felt authentic.

I introduced myself as well. When he heard that my name was Yacoub, he asked where I was from. I told him I was an Arab.

"It's a pleasure meeting you, cousin Yacoub. It is great to have a family member as my neighbor." He said these words in a very genuine and matter-of-fact manner.

At the time, I did not understand what he meant. But later, as I progressed spiritually and intellectually, I more fully comprehended his meaning.

I spent a lot of time with Avraham that year and into the next. The COVID-19 pandemic hit the fitness industry hard, and our gym closed down for several months. I was blessed to have some money saved for hard times like those.

When COVID-19 first struck, I volunteered to help the older folks living in my building with their grocery shopping because they were at higher risk of infection than I was. It turned out that most of the residents in my building were seniors, so I spent a lot of time shopping for food for my neighbors. Avraham was one of them.

In April, my relationship with this gentleman really started to evolve. It was my custom to place the groceries on a table outside his front door, ring the bell, and leave immediately. I kept my distance from him for his own safety.

To my surprise, one day he opened the door instantly when I rang the bell. He asked me if it would be convenient for me to chat with him later that day. He said that he could sit on the far side of his balcony and I could sit on the far side of my balcony so we could keep our distance. I agreed to that arrangement.

My first thought was that the old man must be bored out of his mind and needed someone to visit with. I was entirely unaware at the time that I had found favor in his eyes; Avraham was growing fond of me and wanted to help me realize my true self. I had no clue he saw something in me that I did not see in myself.

Glimmers of Wisdom from the Master

Later that day, when we were sitting on our adjacent balconies, Avraham asked me how I was feeling.

I murmured, "I'm all right, I guess." My tone of voice or body language must have contradicted my words, and he gave me a piercing look. He asked me again how I was *really* doing.

"Well," I replied, "the gym is closed, so I am not making any money, and I cannot even do my workouts. Working out makes me feel good." I sighed. "The fact is, I am not doing very well."

He kept silent for a while and then took a deep breath.

"You know," he said, "if your vision of how life should be coincides with your reality or current life circumstances, then you are happy. However, if your vision of how life should be does not correspond to your reality or current circumstances, then you are unhappy."

Avraham asked me about my vision for my life. I replied that I had had an illustrious vision for myself while I was growing up. With the passage of time, however, my vision had become more and more realistic and reasonable.

He seemed disappointed. In a fatherly manner he said, "What is realistic and reasonable or not should never be a concern of yours. Your mission is just to strive to attain your vision. It is clear to me that you are using your past life experience as a basis for deciding whether or not something is possible.

"Yacoub," he said, "your past does not equal your future, unless you decide to make it so by living in the past. This is harmful to your spirit.

"Humanity is Deity's highest form of creation. We were all created in His image. We are souls having a physical experience, and our souls are striving for expansion and growth.

"Becoming rich spiritually, intellectually, and financially is our human right."

He was silent for a moment and then continued.

"What hasn't happened to you up until now can happen in the future. You are capable of making it happen.

"All you have to do is find your purpose, what you really want out of life, and strive for that. You must be clear about what you really want.

"If you do not know what you want, then how can you create it in your life?

"When you are clear about what you want, you must make a committed decision to attain it. There is no such thing as failure for a person who has made a committed decision.

"Even if you fail a thousand times, there are thousands of lessons to be learned. Successful people fail their way to success.

"Once you commit yourself to creating what you want, then your mind gets organized. When that happens, you can pursue whatever you want.

"What hasn't happened to you up until now *can* happen in the future.

"My friend, you are capable of making it happen, and you should not settle for anything less."

I was amazed by the power of Avraham's words. He was not just speaking words; he was the living embodiment of those words. He spoke with such authority that all doubts were cast from my mind, and I simply knew that this old man was the real deal.

"Everything that we as human beings have created on Earth was essentially first created in our minds," he explained. "That includes both the wonderful things and, sadly, the atrocious things we have created. Both good and evil have come from the human mind.

"It is crucial to cultivate the ability and the will to bring order to your mind. You must have the discipline to do so, or else everything you create in your outer world will be chaotic and disorganized.

"Yacoub, learning to create order in your mind is the basis for creating your world the way you want it to be."

Avraham's statements had captured my full attention, and I had to clarify with a question. "What does 'bringing order to my mind' mean?"

He had a ready answer.

"Bringing order to your mind means organizing your thoughts, emotions, and actions in the direction of attaining your goal and then keeping them organized and steadfast in that direction for a period of time."

"How long is such a period of time?" I asked.

"Until you achieve your goal," Avraham replied.. "You do not stop and you do not quit until you have attained your desire." He added that people get old the minute they give up their visions of the future. "Never give up your vision."

I responded that I had always wanted to live the American dream and be the master of my own destiny. I wanted to be an entrepreneur and own a multimillion-dollar gym.

The Commitment

At that point, Avraham kindly offered to teach me how to realize my vision. He said that knowledge by itself is not power; it is merely potential power. Applied knowledge is the real power.

He then asked if I was willing to make a committed decision to act upon the fundamental tenets of his teachings with faith, and without fear or hesitation.

I agreed to that. But a spoken commitment was not enough for my neighbor. He wanted it in writing. So, on that Sunday early in April, I drafted a commitment document and signed it. On that day, Avraham took a new role in my life. He was no longer the elderly Jewish neighbor next door. From that moment he became my friend, my mentor, and my teacher. In essence, he became my rabbi.

Rabbi Avraham had an abundance of wisdom, knowledge, and energy, which he never failed to share generously with me. As we sat on the far sides of our respective balconies, he taught me, and I listened intently.

He taught me that the way to success, achievement, and fulfillment is self-development and that self-mastery would be the most important work I would ever do. He shared insights with me that engraved themselves into my consciousness and became part of who I was. Those insights became my new, true identity.

My new friend and mentor showed me how to transform myself. And by doing as he taught me, I have been able to transform my life.

As it turned out, Avraham and I did not enjoy the luxury of endless hours together on our balconies. Indeed, our time together was shorter than I could ever have imagined, but it was exquisitely meaningful. This mild-mannered champion of gracious and productive living guided me to a new reality of living, loving, serving, and succeeding beyond my wildest dreams.

His counsel was simple but profound.

"Yacoub," he said, "commit yourself to creating a peaceful, joyful, and loving world both for yourself and for all of mankind. Commit to that, regardless of the ease or difficulty you face."

I committed.

In writing.

1
Integrity

Rabbi Avraham and I agreed to meet regularly on our balconies at 7:00 A.M. Our first session was scheduled for the day before Passover.

I was so excited that I had difficulty falling asleep the night before. Consequently, I overslept that morning and was ten minutes late to our first meeting. I did not pay much attention to my tardiness, but because of it, that morning I received one of the most important lessons of my life.

The Teachings Begin

I sauntered casually outside to my balcony with my notebook, pen, and a cup of hot coffee. Immediately I noticed a troubled expression on Avraham's face. I did not understand why he had such a sad countenance so early in the morning, as I had not seen him like that in the past. My first thought was that he might not be feeling well, and I was concerned.

I asked him if everything was okay. He looked at me gravely and said, "Yacoub, you have a good heart, and that is the only reason I decided to wait for you. You need to understand that time is our most valuable asset, and the way we use it speaks volumes about our personal integrity. I did not expect you to be lacking in this vital quality."

He paused for a moment and looked intently into my eyes. "My friend, you have unlimited potential. But you will never achieve anything worthwhile in your life if you do not possess the most important character trait, which is integrity."

At the time, I truly did not understand why he was making such a fuss. In the Arab culture of my upbringing, being ten minutes late was never frowned upon, and his seemingly harsh judgment raised my defenses.

Rabbi Avraham looked at me in his kind, fatherly way. "Yacoub, do not confuse integrity with morality. Integrity is not so much a matter of morality as it is a matter of workability. Do you know what integrity is?" he asked.

"Of course I do," I replied sharply. "Integrity is doing the right thing when nobody is watching. I always try to do the right thing."

Avraham replied, "My son, there is a deeper motive for integrity. It is about always honoring your word. You might not be able always to *keep* your word, but you can definitely always *honor* your word.

"If you cannot keep your word for some reason or another, you must always take responsibility and communicate promptly that you cannot keep your word. That way you will have honored your word."

I did not understand what Avraham was saying. My anger prevented me from listening. I was hearing the words, but I was not listening.

"Yacoub," he insisted, "you need to listen very carefully.

Things might happen in life that are outside your control and may hinder you from keeping your word.

"When such a thing happens, you must immediately communicate with the person to whom you gave your word and explain the circumstances. In that way, though you could not keep your word, you have honored your word, which is more valuable than all the wealth and success in the world."

As I grappled with that new idea, Rabbi Avraham continued, "I am not chastising you, Yacoub. I am simply observing a habitual pattern within you that is holding you back from being the splendid person you truly are."

There was something about his tone of voice that spoke to my spirit, and I apologized for being late to our meeting. He immediately smiled and said, "Now that integrity has been restored, we can move forward.

"The first lesson I want you to learn is this very important insight about integrity. Success in all your transactions and undertakings can only be established on the rock-solid foundation of integrity. Without it, you have nothing. You must always honor your word.

"Yacoub, honesty is telling the truth. Integrity is creating your world with your word. Integrity must be at the center of your life. It must be the source of your power, security, leadership, and self-worth."

A Burning Question

I nodded and was silent for a bit. Then I gathered my courage and said, "Rabbi, there is something I would like to ask you."

"Anything," he replied.

My words pierced the mild morning air. "Do you think

there will ever be peace in the Middle East?"

Raised eyebrows accompanied by a soft "oh my!" were his initial reaction, but after a few moments he smiled placidly and responded. "Yacoub, I will be happy to tell you what I think. But first I will give you my short answer."

He straightened himself in his chair and began to speak.

"During my long life of interacting with fellow travelers in this mortal realm, I have come to understand and value the extraordinary resilience of the human spirit. The remarkable ability of the human spirit to embrace principles of truth, love, respect, and eternal progress has given me enormous hope for the future.

"Unlikely though it may seem at the moment, my heart tells me to believe that when leaders of true integrity come together, desiring trust and unity in their purposes, it could be possible for them to listen to one another with pure intent, creating understanding and agreement far beyond ordinary ideas and opinions.

"If our two beloved peoples should ever achieve such enlightenment, then yes, I feel certain it could result in a peaceful resolution of the conflict."

He leaned back in his chair, signaling the close of that part of our conversation.

"Wow," I breathed. "So much to think about."

"Indeed," he said. "Shall we dig a little deeper?"

"Be my guest," I responded. Now it was my turn to straighten my back. I gave him my full attention.

Pursuing Peace

"Shakespeare wrote, 'To thine own self be true,'" Rabbi

Avraham began. "We must be true to ourselves and to others. If we look at peacemaking in terms of winning and losing, then we have lost sight of authentic peace.

"Yacoub, we must have inner peace before we can achieve outer peace. Only when people make peace within themselves will they be able to make peace in the outer world.

"In terms of global conflict, we are living in a chaotic world. The Middle East has been engulfed in war for a very long time, and we see tensions between Israel and its neighboring countries. We also see the Shia-Sunni divide, which has grown into hatred."

Rabbi Avraham paused, deep in his thoughts, and then continued.

"A nineteenth-century rabbi interpreted the closing verse of the book of Malachi. It tells of reconciliation between parents and their children as a vision of hope for a future relationship between Judaism and the other Abrahamic religions. We must work together to make this vision a reality.

"The sages say, 'Seek peace and pursue it,' and that must be our life's goal every day. We start with peace within ourselves, and then we extend that peace to our outer world. Peace is a state of mind and a state of being. It means encouraging shared values and working for the common good of all.

"Individuals at peace within themselves rise above their pain and find the inner strength to transform their painful moments into wisdom. We must make a committed decision to seek peace and pursue it in order to heal broken relationships.

"The Talmud says that turning an enemy into a friend

is one of the highest *mitzvoth,* or commandments, we can accomplish, and that means putting one's pride on the line for the greater good of mankind.

"Make no mistake about it: peacemaking is a laborious task. It takes hard work and patience, whether we are talking about inner or outer peace.

"Peace is a very important belief in the Abrahamic religions. Jews greet each other by saying *shalom.* And as you know, Arabs use the word *salaam.* Both terms are used to mean both *hello* and *goodbye.* However, the real meaning of both *shalom* and *salaam* is peace, harmony, and prosperity. Peace is the essence of the Abrahamic religions."

Rabbi Avraham remarked, "You might also be interested to know that when the Islamic armies of the prophet Muhammad entered Jerusalem, not a single person was killed because of his faith."

He then spoke of Saint Francis of Assisi, a thirteenth-century Italian mystic and preacher who was a symbol of peace. Closing his eyes, Avraham tenderly delivered the powerful, heartfelt prayer ascribed to that long-ago saint:

Lord, make me an instrument of your peace.
Where there is hatred, let me sow love.
Where there is offense, let me bring pardon.
Where there is discord, let me bring union.
Where there is error, let me bring truth.
Where there is doubt, let me bring faith.
Where there is despair, let me bring hope.
Where there is darkness, let me bring your light.
Where there is sadness, let me bring joy.

After my rabbi recited those powerful words, he opened his eyes and saw that I was deeply pondering what I had just heard. I was moved, touched, and inspired. The words he had delivered straight from his heart to mine permeated every cell of my being.

Listening without Limiting

As Rabbi Avraham spoke, I was actively listening and capturing his words in writing. Noticing my intense interest, he seemed to change his focus somewhat.

"Yacoub," he observed, "there is a big dilemma with most people in the world. They usually do not listen."

"Rabbi," I replied, sensing that something important was coming, "I am eager to listen to your wisdom."

"That is because you are a humble seeker," he said. "Most people seek only information that confirms what they already believe.

"Sadly, people often do not hear what is really being said. They hear what they want to hear. If it contradicts what they already believe, they argue against it. Their response has nothing to do with the validity of what is being said but everything to do with their own beliefs and worldview."

He added, "People unconsciously develop limiting beliefs about themselves and the world which affect their decision-making and their actions, causing them to miss out on great opportunities.

"Successful people make a committed decision not to allow their environment or past results to shape their beliefs. They create their own empowering beliefs.

"Nelson Mandela was a great example of that principle.

He was imprisoned for a quarter of a century, but he did not play the victim or blame others. He decided that the environment in South Africa at the time was not going to dictate what he would believe. The rest is history. He became the first black president of his beloved South Africa."

As Rabbi Avraham spoke about limiting beliefs, I pondered the thought that many Arabs might not be willing to speak with Israelis because of their own limiting beliefs about Jews.

My rabbi saw that I had stopped writing and asked me if I understood what he was saying. When I shared with him what I was thinking, he commented wistfully, "There are likewise numerous Jews who have limiting beliefs about Arabs."

"Well," I retorted with a small grin, "I am certainly glad, sir, that you are not one of them. Otherwise, I wouldn't be able to sponge some of your Passover matzah balls off you!"

Avraham's laugh blossomed into an enormous belly laugh. I laughed at his laughter, and our laughing quickly became loud and uncontrollable. Laughter can be very infectious. Then, still smiling, the good rabbi observed, "Our neighbors are wondering what these two *mashuganas* are up to!"

That was my first lesson with Rabbi Avraham—and what a lesson it was! With great anticipation I looked forward to our next time together. I wanted to impress him by being there early to show that I was a good student.

2

Success

I had been pondering the words of Rabbi Avraham and could hardly wait until our next encounter. It was scheduled for the Sunday after Passover.

That morning I made sure I was ten minutes early, and he seemed very glad to see me. He mentioned that he had prepared some matzah balls for me and would leave them on the little table outside the front door of his apartment.

Chuckling, he added, "Don't worry. I used a healthy oil."

We laughed together.

The Magic of Goals and Ideals

Now it was time to get down to business. My rabbi started by firing a question at me. "Yacoub, do you know what success is?"

Without hesitation I replied, "To be wealthy."

Just as quickly, he corrected me. "Earl Nightingale, an American radio speaker and author, defined success as the progressive realization of a worthy ideal."

I was puzzled, so I shot my own question back to him. "What is a worthy ideal?"

"Well," he explained, "an ideal does not have to be about money. Think of the schoolteacher in a rural area who wants to provide his or her students with the best education possible. Or the mother who wants to provide the best care for her children and raise them to become honest and productive citizens. A worthy ideal is whatever the individual perceives as a worthy ideal.

"Yacoub, it is very important to have goals and worthy ideals. If you don't know where you're heading, the chances are you'll never get anywhere, and you will live your life simply going through the motions.

"In my experience," Rabbi Avraham continued, "life gives us exactly what we ask from it. Therefore, the first thing to do is to ask for exactly what you want. If your request is vague, whatever you achieve will be muddled. If you don't ask for anything, you won't get anything. Your goal must be definite and precise.

"Always remember that it is not just about achieving your goal. It is about who you become along the way.

"Goals are not only about making things happen; they are about growing and raising your awareness of life. Most self-made millionaires and billionaires are happiest on their way to their goals, before they ever actually attain them. We human beings are always happiest when we are making progress in our lives."

As Rabbi Avraham spoke, I was incessantly taking notes. Throughout our times together, I took prolific notes.

He posed another question. "Why do some people with goals follow through, whereas others do not?"

I wanted to give a good answer that would impress my

teacher. After a few moments, I had the perfect response.

As if I had just invented the wheel, I declared proudly, "Because of a lack of resources."

A subtle upward quirk of the rabbi's lip told me that he was stifling a laugh as he observed that I was trying to impress him with my answer.

"Yacoub," he said quietly, "success and getting rich are never about resources. They are about *being resourceful.*"

While I was considering that sage observation, he added a few layers of thought-provoking insight.

Roadblocks and Roadways to Success

"People may choose not to follow through with their goals and ideals because of three main reasons," the good rabbi pointed out. "First, they do not have a big enough *why*. When people have a significant goal, too often they waste their time thinking about *how* they are going to achieve it, and they give up before they even start. They need to focus on the *why* and not the *how*.

"People with a big enough *why* generally persevere and follow through, while people with a feeble *why* quit at the first sign of challenge or defeat. Simply put, if they have a big enough *why*, the *how* will take care of itself in due time."

His summary was dynamic: "The only prerequisite for any person to attain anything they desire in life is to really, really want it. And they need to have a big enough *why*."

Of course, he was just getting started.

"Fear is the second reason people do not persevere and follow through on an inspired thought or idea. The fearful mindset often passes from generation to generation as a survival mechanism. It is useful for us to survive, but it does not help us to thrive. Too often fear prevents us from taking action toward the fulfillment of our goals."

Rabbi Avraham noted that some people are too afraid to enter the metaphorical cave that quite often holds the very treasures they are passionately seeking.

"There is nothing we can do to take the fear away," he concluded. "The only way to overcome fear is to face it.

"Yacoub," he asked, "what is the opposite of fear?"

This time I hesitated to answer him but managed to squeak out, "Courage."

He responded with another keen insight and a firm challenge: "The opposite of fear is faith. Both faith and fear require us to believe in something we cannot see. From this moment onward, I want you always to choose faith over fear."

Rabbi Avraham taught me that successful people are afraid, but they do not let fear stop them. Instead, they follow through because they are more afraid of what life would be if they *don't* follow through. They are actually terrified of settling for the status quo, which would mean just hoping that one day things might change for the better by mere chance or circumstance.

"The third reason people do not follow through is their negative belief systems," he explained. "Most people have enormous potential. Some fully tap into it, but sadly, some do not.

"People with healthy self-beliefs reach their potential by taking massive action. Based on the law of cause and effect, which states that every action causes an equal reaction, their massive action produces massive results and reinforces their strong sense of self-efficacy. Consequently, they take even more massive action and produce even greater results. This upward spiral is how the rich get richer.

"People who have poor self-beliefs, on the other hand, might have boundless potential, but because of their negative beliefs about their abilities, they tap even less of that potential, take even less action, and produce even worse results. That is a downward spiral, and sadly enough, it is how the poor get poorer."

The rabbi was firm in his next statement.

"Yacoub, if you don't think you can become rich and successful, you likely won't. You must begin by *believing* that you can.

"All the wise thinkers agree that the greatest limitations are those which individuals impose upon themselves. Always remember that your success starts with your mindset and beliefs. You must *believe* in order to *achieve*."

The Most Potent Secret

As I was pondering what Rabbi Avraham had just said to me, I began to feel great yearnings for positive self-belief and success. After a long silence, I asked, "Rabbi, how can I strengthen my faith? How can I obtain confidence and believe that I will realize my vision of a successful life?"

He received my questions with a kind smile and insightful answers.

"First of all, in order to be wealthy, you must have a burning desire to be rich spiritually, intellectually, and temporally. You must then supplement your desire with faith. You have to *believe* that you will become wealthy."

His comments caused me frustration, and I interrupted.

"But how? How can I have faith in achieving something that I have never achieved in my life? How can I have faith in producing abundance when everything about my current circumstances points toward lack and economic challenges?"

His voice was firm as he offered a one-sentence solution.

"You can obtain faith through the repetition of words."

"Repetition of words?" I muttered. Was this for real?

"Yes, my son," the rabbi confirmed. "We create our world with our words. Words are very powerful. Their power is so great that they don't even need to be true to have an effect on our subconscious minds."

I wondered how that could be true.

"You see, Yacoub," he continued, "the mind consists of two parts, the conscious mind and the subconscious mind. The conscious mind is called the intellectual mind or the thinking mind. It has the ability to choose to accept or reject any thought or idea that is presented to it.

"The subconscious mind, on the other hand, is called the emotional mind. It does not have the ability to choose to accept or reject anything. Whatever is fed to the subconscious mind, accompanied by intense emotion, it must absolutely accept."

My interest deepened as he continued.

"Although the subconscious mind does not have the ability to choose to accept or reject, it is actually much more powerful than the conscious mind. Your subconscious mind guides and controls your entire life. Your habitual patterns and self-image reside in your subconscious mind.

"The good news is that your subconscious mind is extremely vulnerable to the power of emotionalized words. You must learn how to control it and make it serve you and work for you, not the other way around. Otherwise, it will dominate every facet of your life without your permission.

"Now, here is the key," Avraham insisted. "The only way to influence your subconscious mind is through the repetition of words. This technique is commonly called autosuggestion or affirmation. Of course, it is more powerful and beneficial if you say your affirmations loudly and with an abundance of emotion."

He informed me that Émile Coué, a French psychologist and pharmacist, had popularized the autosuggestion method of self-improvement in the early 1920s. It was characterized by frequent repetition of the formula sentence "Every day, and in every way, I am getting better and better."

Rabbi Avraham explained further. "Your affirmation must have four components. It must be personal, positive, present tense, and emotional. For example, you could repeat an affirmation like this: 'I am grateful that I am the owner of a multimillion-dollar gym, and I provide the best care and service to my customers.'

"'I am grateful'—*that's the emotional*—'that I'—*that's the personal*—'am'—*present tense*—'the owner of a multimillion-dollar gym, and I provide the best care and service to my customers'—*that's the positive.*"

My rabbi looked at me closely. "I know this might seem simple, and indeed it is simple, but it is definitely not *easy,* because your old programming and self-image will put up a mighty fight.

"But let me tell you that success is guaranteed if you persist. *That is the most potent secret on the face of the earth.*"

The Power of Affirmations

He paused for a moment to let this statement sink into my soul, and then he continued with a certain fervency.

"Yacoub, remember that each one of us is subject to affirmations throughout our lives. Every day we are influenced by outward suggestions and information from the news, the media, and the environment.

"Each of us is also influenced by an inner monologue. Some of us repeat to ourselves that we will never be successful because we come from a disadvantaged ancestry, or because we have had failures in our past, or because we don't have enough money, resources, skills, or intelligence. We drift from one failure to the next—not because we don't have the necessary qualities to succeed, but because we have been constantly telling ourselves we are failures, and that is how we subconsciously see ourselves."

Avraham's gaze seemed to penetrate my being. "My dear Yacoub, for many years you have been putting limitations on yourself with disempowering words. But you must now begin to pay close attention to the words you tell yourself *about* yourself.

"Please understand that every experience or thought you have ever had, every word you have ever heard, has become permanently engraved in your subconscious mind. Without your realizing it, your past experiences and words have convinced you that you are not the type of person who can become an entrepreneur, a successful gym owner, and a multimillionaire, even though you do in fact have all the potential to be that person."

At this point I was feeling overwhelmed, and I protested.

"But how in the world can I ever change myself just by—"

He raised his hand to silence me.

"Even if you don't believe in the power of affirmations in the beginning, I want you to do them anyway," he said. "After a period of time, this technique will begin acting upon you. The more you internalize an affirmation, the more powerful it becomes. Just remember to base your judgment of whether or not it works on the results you will be getting, rather than on intellectual reasoning."

He further explained this unique process.

"If you want to change your outer world and circumstances, you must change your inner self. All the outer details of your life reflect what is inside you, including your thoughts, ideas, emotions, and self-image. And, Yacoub, you can *never* overachieve your self-image. It is so powerful that it becomes your destiny."

"Rabbi," I admitted, "I have always cared about the good opinion of others, and I try to hide my lack of confidence by having a muscular build."

His affection was evident as he replied, "My friend, you can change your self-image. You must be aware that your self-image is in your subconscious mind, which can be influenced at will. Through the power of affirmations, you have the ability to create a new self-image and convince your subconscious mind that you can obtain absolutely anything and everything you want.

"In fact, you can convince your subconscious mind that you are already in possession of the qualities and success you want to create in your life by acting *now* like the person you want to become. The subconscious mind will accept your newly created self-image in the same way it accepted your old self-image.

"I will also remind you that your self-image was not formed exclusively by you. It was largely formed when you were a child, when your subconscious mind was especially susceptible. Each suggestion you accepted during those younger years, even though it may have been totally false, penetrated your subconscious and became part of your self-image.

"You must remember that although your current self-image was not formed solely by you, you still must take responsibility for it. That is the only way to change or transform something.

"It is not possible to change anything by playing the victim and blaming your outer circumstances, parents, or environment. You can change your self-image only after you take responsibility for it."

From Past to Present: A New Vision

As I listened to Avraham's description of the subconscious mind and its importance in blocking or enabling success, my mind was suddenly drawn back to a long-ago incident that related directly to his conversation. Was this experience an influencer that I hadn't fully understood before? I believe it began a subconscious pattern that needed now to be addressed.

It was a hot summer day in Beirut, Lebanon. I was five years old and had gone to the seashore with my parents, eager to play in the kids' pool by the beach.

I spent most of the morning frolicking in the pool and

then ran over to the table where my parents were having lunch. I devoured my meal, but my real focus was on getting back to the pool.

A few minutes later, I headed to what I thought was the kids' pool. I still vividly remember how beautiful the blue sky was as I sat at the pool's edge and prepared to hurl myself into the cool, refreshing water.

But it was far from a casual plunge. To my surprise, my feet did not touch the bottom of the pool, and I found myself sinking deeper and deeper into the water. There was nothing solid under my feet. Suddenly, panic began to overtake me as I felt my lungs screaming for air.

Later, I realized I had mistakenly jumped into the adults' pool. But in that moment, I just wanted to get to the surface and be able to breathe. It was a matter of survival.

For long, agonizing moments I kept fighting and swallowing water. When I finally reached the surface, I clung to the pool's edge with all my strength, coughing up what seemed like gallons of water. My heart was pounding wildly.

After several minutes I was able to climb out of the pool. But in the midst of that terrifying experience, my life had changed forever. It was as if my little five-year-old self had in that moment set me on a course that could easily have prevented me from achieving any form of success.

What that five-year-old voice said to me was, "Yacoub, *be careful* before you leap. Yacoub, *be cautious* before you jump. Yacoub, *you must be very, very wary about everything.*"

My subconscious mind had heard and believed that message, and from then on, I seemed doomed to a life barely beyond survival. I let fear dictate my decisions. But now, remembering that incident as a grown man under the tutelage of an inspired adviser, I realized that with work and a vigorous new self-image, I could begin to understand and appreciate the true gifts of life without being dominated by fear. Fear had helped me survive, but it had never helped me thrive.

A whole new world had been opened to my vision. I felt confident that Rabbi Avraham would be able to guide me through the steps to true success.

Studying, Understanding, Being, Creating

Avraham's next comment brought me quickly back to the present as he continued on a more personal note.

"You know," he observed, "I have been working on my own self-image for decades. I am an avid reader. I wake up every morning at 4:00 A.M. to read and study.

"In addition to the Torah, I have read hundreds of other books, including biographies and written works of great world leaders and thinkers: Abraham Lincoln, Benjamin Franklin, Socrates, Wallace Wattles, and Stephen Covey, to name only a few."

He smiled a bit in reminiscence. Then he turned again to me and my unique mission. I sensed that our day's discussion was drawing to a close.

"Yacoub," he said, "your most important effort is to act and feel *now* as the person you want to be. Many people think that they have to *do* in order to *have,* and when they *have,* then they will *be.* But this is not how the creation cycle works.

"In order to create something great in your life, first and foremost you must *be* that person *now.* Then you believe and act in accordance with that new identity or self-image, and you will *have* the things that you desire. In other words, the creation cycle is not *doing-having-being;* it is *being-doing-having.* We are not human *do*-ings; we are human *be*-ings."

Rabbi Avraham asked me pointedly, "Yacoub, are you willing to start working on your self-image by being that person *now*?"

I took a deep breath and replied. "I am, dear sir. I will start reading and doing affirmations, but it will be hard for me to wake up at 4:00 every morning. I will start by waking up at 5:00 A.M. But which book should I start reading?"

Rabbi Avraham chuckled. "I will leave a couple of books on the table next to the matzah balls. I have been continually reading these books for years now, and it is time for them to have a new owner. One who appreciates them."

He recommended that I read for one hour every morning and then look into a mirror and boldly repeat affirmations for ten minutes in the morning and again in the evening.

That afternoon I received a text from my teacher saying that the food he had prepared for me was ready. I went next door and found a huge plate of matzah balls on the small table outside his front door. Next to it was a plastic bag containing books.

I was excited to see the books Rabbi Avraham had given me. First was an old leather-bound book: *Think and Grow Rich—The Complete Text,* by Napoleon Hill. The other volume was *The Power of Now,* by Eckhart Tolle.

I took the books and the food inside my apartment, holding the volumes eagerly to my chest. The matzah balls were delicious, and I devoured every last bite. I did not care about the calories or the sodium content. It was a meal prepared for me by my teacher, and that was the only thing that mattered.

3

Attitude of Gratitude

I began waking up every morning at 5:00 A.M. My morning ritual consisted of reading for one hour and then for ten minutes repeating my affirmation in front of the mirror: "I am grateful that I am the owner of a multimillion-dollar gym, and I provide the best care and service to my customers."

I must say, it felt weird in the beginning. However, I remembered Rabbi Avraham's counsel not to base my judgment on intellectual reasoning.

Daily Thanksgiving

Rabbi Avraham also instructed me to repeat my affirmation with intense emotion and deep feelings of gratitude.

"Yacoub," he advised, "you must live with gratitude in your heart on a daily basis. A grateful heart expects good things, and you must always have feelings of gratitude in order to retain a long-lasting faith.

"Practicing this virtue means recognizing the good that is already yours."

My teacher reminded me that virtually all religions attest to the importance of gratitude:

"The Hebrew expression for gratitude is *hakarat hatov,* which literally means 'recognizing the good.'

"In Catholicism, the word *eucharist* derives from the Greek word *eucharistia,* meaning 'thanksgiving.'

"Martin Luther referred to gratitude as 'the basic Christian attitude.'

"And the Islamic sacred text, the Quran, is brimming with the idea of gratitude. It encourages its followers to express thanks in all circumstances."

The Tougher the Challenge, the Greater the Gift

"Yacoub," Avraham urged with a fervent depth of feeling, "you must nurture the habit of being grateful for *everything* in your life."

I was taken aback by his intensity and wondered if he really understood my challenges.

I asked, "Do you mean I should even be grateful for the very tough problems I have in my life right now? Look, Rabbi, I am not working, and who knows when I will be able to go back to work again. My life's savings are dwindling rapidly, and I may never be able to replenish them. How do you expect me to be grateful for *everything?*"

He responded calmly. "Let me ask you something. When you work out at the gym, do you use the same weights every time, or do you gradually increase them? Do you push yourself in your workouts, or do you just go through the motions? Judging by your build, I would say that you continuously push yourself. Am I right?"

"Yes, you are right," I replied, wondering what he would say next.

He continued, "Well, problems exist to help you develop your mental and spiritual muscles. Each challenge is a gift, and I believe the difficulty you just mentioned is a gift. It has enabled us to spend time together, allowed me to share my knowledge with you, and provided you with the space and time to dig deep into yourself and discover what you're truly capable of. So yes, indeed, you must always be grateful for everything in your life."

In retrospect, I could see that Rabbi Avraham was right. I had been pushing and training my physical body with strenuous workouts, and it felt great. "No pain, no gain" was my mantra at the gym. I realized that the time had now come for me to start training my intellectual and spiritual muscles.

The Root of All Evil?

I asked, "Rabbi, how did you make your money?"

He corrected me with a twinkle in his eye. "I did not make my money. I earned it. People who *make* money are in jail."

We laughed together, and then my rabbi shared with me some important insights.

"Yacoub," he said, "to accumulate wealth, you need to have a good relationship with money. Some people think that money is the root of all evil. That is simply a misunderstanding.

"Money is a tool that was created to facilitate trade. You have to learn to use it and get it to work for you. Money should never use you, or else it is going to work against you.

"Money allows you to do good in the world. You can't give to charity or feed the poor without money. Being generous fosters generosity, so you must willingly give."

I sensed that I had much to learn.

He pressed on. "You need to spend your money on things that increase, not decrease, in value. Each dollar is like a loyal soldier. Spend your money buying assets, not liabilities.

"Buying assets is when you send out your dollars, or soldiers, and they bring more dollars, or soldiers, back to you. Buying liabilities is when you send out your soldiers and they do not return to you. It is as simple as that. Throughout my life, I've been acquiring assets and avoiding liabilities.

"The greatest investment you can ever make is investing in yourself and others. The Talmud says, 'A person should divide his money into thirds: a third in hard assets, a third in liquid assets, and a third in semi-liquid assets.' That is sound financial advice no matter what your religion is.

"Strive always to keep things in perspective and remember the words of Earl Nightingale: 'Success is not the result of making money; earning money is the result of success, and success is in direct proportion to your service.'"

Multiple Streams of Income

His next observation seemed crucial to understanding success.

"Yacoub, the money you earn will always be in direct proportion, first, to the need for what you do; second, your ability to do it; and third, the degree of difficulty there is in replacing you.

"Trading your time for money will never make you really rich. It will only provide you with a basic level of security. Most people trade their time for money, and that is the reason they do not become financially independent. In order to become really wealthy, you must have multiple sources of income."

I felt a complaint rising in my throat. "But how? It is very hard for me to comprehend how I can have multiple sources of income when I currently do not have a single one."

Rabbi Avraham nodded. "You are saying that because you have been programmed to use your senses only as you consider your current circumstances. You are forming images in your mind of your lack of financial means. Then you are getting emotionally involved with these negative images and impressing them upon your subconscious mind.

"Because your subconscious mind controls all your actions, you end up engaging in the same old behaviors and hence creating the same life circumstances. What you need to do, my friend, is to start using your imagination, which is one of your higher intellectual faculties."

"My imagination," I muttered.

Avraham nodded. "Yes, Yacoub, your imagination. Did you know Albert Einstein said that imagination is more important than knowledge?"

I confessed that I did not.

Imagine That

The rabbi stood up to refocus my attention on him. "Yacoub, I want you to listen carefully. You must start using your imagination to break the cycle of creating the same difficulties over and over again in your life. And you have to stop looking at your current circumstances!"

I knew he meant business when he declared, "Your starting point must be a vision of the life you want to create for yourself. Begin now to form images of what you want to happen, and start getting emotionally involved with those images. Such practices will impress the images onto your subconscious mind, helping you to create empowering results corresponding with your new vision."

What Rabbi Avraham had said made complete sense. Indeed, thus far I had been playing it safe and never stretched myself beyond my senses.

But he was far from finished with his lesson.

"I want you to make a vision board," he said. "I want you to put pictures on that board of your multimillion-dollar gym. I want you to add pictures of the house or condo that you want to own and not just rent, the car you want to drive, the countries you want to visit, and anything else you desire."

He added a little practical advice.

"You can find such pictures all over the internet. You can even Photoshop them and put them on your vision board. Then look at them many times daily and let your imagination soar. Your results will be spectacular!"

After trying to digest my teacher's detailed instructions and promise of success, I found myself deep in thought—and not in a positive way. Contemplating the multitude of new daily rituals I was getting myself into, I breathed a heavy sigh and looked crossly at him.

"I am no longer sleeping in," I grumbled. "I am waking up at 5:00 A.M. every day. I am spending a full hour studying first thing in the morning. I am repeating my affirmations loudly in front of a mirror twice a day. And now you want me to put together a vision board and start relying on my imagination like a little child?

"Until very recently, all I cared about was training my clients at the gym, working out, having my five healthy meals a day, and competing in powerlifting events. To tell you the truth, I was more comfortable living like that."

I sullenly slumped back against my chair and stared at my knees.

Rabbi Avraham did not hesitate. Pointedly he asked, "Yacoub, you were a little more comfortable then. But were you fulfilled?"

After a moment or two, I murmured faintly, "Well, I guess . . . uh, no."

His next words were cautionary. "My friend, if you take the easy road, the challenges in your life will only get bigger, and you will never be fulfilled."

The Last of the Human Freedoms

My rabbi asked me if I knew who Victor Frankl was.

"Wasn't he an author or something?" I asked.

Rabbi Avraham responded, "Viktor Frankl was an Austrian psychiatrist and psychotherapist who was imprisoned in four different concentration camps, including Auschwitz, during World War II. In addition to all the cruelty and suffering he had to endure himself, his parents, brother, and pregnant wife all perished in the camps.

"After the war, he wrote a book entitled *Man's Search for Meaning*. In that extraordinary book, he stated that everything can be taken from a person but one thing: the last of the human freedoms, which is to choose one's attitude in any given set of circumstances."

He spoke to me in subdued but intense tones. "My friend, your attitude is a combination of your thoughts, emotions, and actions. You need to keep your moods and behavior in check. You must always have a positive attitude toward life, events, and people. Your ultimate success will depend on it."

I was silent as he continued.

"My dear young friend, so filled with infinite potential and longing to achieve it, I cannot emphasize strongly enough how important your attitude is if you really want to live a worthy life and realize your true destiny.

"When you start a new task, your attitude will determine whether or not you enjoy the journey and finish it successfully. Regardless of the circumstances, you can always choose your attitude—right or wrong, positive or negative. If you have a positive attitude toward life and others, you will find that they have the same positive attitude toward you.

"Yacoub, you can absolutely go as far and as high as you desire if you develop and maintain an enthusiastic attitude. That is because such an attitude is faith in action, and it will never betray you."

Choice of a Lifetime

He was silent for a long moment as his piercing blue eyes caught and held my attention. When he spoke again, I was stunned.

"Now, before we continue with our meetings," he said, "you must make a committed decision always to maintain a positive, enthusiastic attitude. If you will not or cannot do this, there is no need for us to continue our meetings. I will always be your friend, but I will stop being your teacher."

Suddenly I was breathless, as breathless as that five-year-old boy struggling for air in the swimming pool so many years before. How could I survive even the thought of losing Rabbi Avraham as my mentor?

Here was a man in his eighties, sitting on his side of his balcony, selflessly and patiently sharing his time and wisdom with me. For some reason he had believed in me, and in that moment, I knew I must step up and develop the new patterns and behaviors he was recommending.

"Rabbi Avraham," I declared with deep emotion, "I do not want to lose you as my teacher."

A tentative smile hovered shyly upon his lips. "Very well, Yacoub. If you want to achieve the same results that I have enjoyed, all you have to do is follow the example of what I have done, and your success is guaranteed. If I can create the life I love, so can you. But it is essential to do everything exactly as I tell you to do it. Are you willing to make a committed decision to do so?"

Without the slightest hesitation, I offered my pledge. "I am willing, Rabbi. I will do it!"

4

Taking Action and Living in the Now

After my most recent session with Rabbi Avraham, I was more determined than ever to master the awesome teachings he was sharing with me.

During our conversations, he reminded me that he had acquired much of his vast knowledge and expertise from the books he had read and the self-development seminars he had attended. He had made sizeable investments in himself, to the tune of tens of thousands of dollars spent on treasured books, seminars, and a variety of inspiring and educational opportunities.

The good news, he said, was that he made great returns on his investments while he pursued his amazing journey of becoming a self-made multimillionaire. He was not saying that to sing his own praises but rather to impress upon me that I must continually study, learn, take action, and grow.

Beginnings

My rabbi told me that the first self-development book he had ever read was the book he had given me: *Think and Grow Rich,* by Napoleon Hill. He also shared fond memories of listening to his first inspirational speaker, Earl Nightingale, who had recorded *The Strangest Secret* back in 1956.

Avraham was twenty years old at the time, living paycheck to paycheck and barely making ends meet when he started his quest for financial independence. Inspired by the book and the recording, he moved immediately into action and started applying what he had learned. That was when the transformation began.

Over time, his life and outer circumstances started to magically change because his awareness and money consciousness had been dramatically altered. He began to invest in real estate, buying duplexes, triplexes, and fourplexes. The rest, as they say, was history.

Rabbi Avraham shared with me that his beloved wife, Helen, had passed away four years before, and his two sons, Daniel and Joshua, were taking care of his hundred-plus properties spread throughout New York and Florida.

After young Avraham got a taste of success back in the 1960s, reading and studying became his daily ritual. He also made sure he attended a minimum of two seminars every year. During our sessions together, his eyes lit up as he mentioned some of those speakers: Zig Ziglar, Bob Proctor, and Tony Robbins. He was genuinely fond of each one of them.

Rabbi Avraham said that what these valuable books and renowned speakers represented to him was not merely philosophies or intellectual discourses. The values and insights he learned represented the map and direction he needed to arrive at the destination he had set for himself.

Hard Work, Risk, Discomfort, and Action

During our next meeting, the rabbi taught me the importance of hard work and taking action.

"Yacoub," he said, "merely *talking* and *asking* will never get your prayers answered. Prayers are answered according to your faith as you take action.

"When you want something to happen with every cell of your being, you must take immediate action. People waste time waiting for all the perfect conditions to fall into place and never get anything accomplished. Being careful is sometimes good and might help you avoid certain mistakes, but being overly cautious after obtaining all the facts is a big mistake.

"People who hesitate and refuse to take risks never achieve their full potential. All self-made millionaires failed their way to success. In order to succeed, you must step boldly into uncertainty and discomfort. It is said that the only way to take over an island is to burn your ships and cut off your exits. Only then can you mobilize all your inner powers."

My teacher must have sensed something amiss in my demeanor. He stopped and asked, "What's wrong, Yacoub?"

In a defeated tone of voice I confessed, "Rabbi, I have not yet taken any action with respect to owning my own gym."

His eyes widened as he shook his head. "On the contrary," he objected vigorously. "You have most definitely taken action. You are reading, studying, repeating your affirmations, and doing your visualizations. You must trust the process, and the inspired result will soon follow.

"Always remember what 'honest Abe' said: 'If I had five minutes to chop down a tree, I'd spend the first three sharpening my axe.' You are currently doing what the great president of our beautiful country said he would do. You are sharpening your axe.

"In the Torah, it is written: 'Whatever task comes your way to do, do it with all your strength.' Similar statements are written in your Holy Book as well. Therefore, you should never have a Plan B. If you have a Plan B, your Plan A is guaranteed to fail."

I was shocked. Thus far, I had always put a Plan B in place for each Plan A. But now I was beginning to understand why each Plan A had seldom worked. It was quite a revelation!

The rabbi noticed that I was feeling overwhelmed, and he offered some caring counsel.

"Yacoub, do not spend your time today thinking about possible future emergencies. You must have faith that you are capable of surmounting any challenges when they arrive. Simply take action, and do every day's work to the fullest. It is not about the quantity but about the quality of your work.

"If you do each task in an effective and efficient manner every day, I can promise you a successful life. Most importantly," he added with conviction, "remember that the best time for action is *now*."

When Action Meets Now

We met again a few days later, and Rabbi Avraham seemed eager to continue our discussion.

"You will remember," he said, "that the last word I said to you last time was *now*."

I nodded, recalling the end of our wide-ranging conversation.

"Today," he smiled, "I would like to revisit that tiny but illustrious word in all its glory."

I was a bit puzzled but certainly willing to take the plunge.

"Yes, I would enjoy that," I responded.

"You see, at that time we talked about the importance of Now as it relates to taking bold and appropriate action to achieve goals. But I wish to speak with you today about Now as an actual way of living—a means of realizing your full potential."

"Well, that could be very useful," I mused.

"Good!" he exclaimed, and I knew it would be an interesting morning.

"So here is the thing," he began, like a child about to share a burning secret with his best friend. "Yacoub, you *must* learn to live in the *here and now,* not dwelling on the past or the future."

I looked at him encouragingly.

"It is a matter of mental concentration, really," he explained. "Energy flows powerfully toward what you focus on, so always concentrate on your vision and the good you want to create in your life. The more you focus on what you are doing, absorbed in the person or task before you, the more you live in the present moment. Hence, focus and concentration are some of the most important keys to success."

His voice rose a notch as he continued. "I repeat: Ensure that your awareness is completely centered on the Now. Do not fret about the future or agonize over the past. When you live in the Now, you are living where life is unfolding and responding to your deepest desires. That is exactly where you want to be at all times."

Rabbi Avraham summarized with gusto. "It is evident," he insisted, "that every action you take must be taken in the Now. You cannot act in the past, so it behooves you to dismiss the past from your mind. Also, you cannot act in the future, because it is not here yet. Or if you act in the Now and your mind is focused on either the past or the future, your present action will collide with your divided attention and will not be effective.

"Yacoub, you must put your whole mind and energy into your present action. Hold tight to your vision and life's purpose, always focusing on the actions you are taking today. Live in the Now."

Forgive and Embrace the Moment

While I was grappling with the intricacies of living in the Now, the good rabbi added yet another dimension to that fascinating concept.

"My son," he counseled, "in order to be able to live in the Now, you must forgive. That means letting go of all improprieties and resentments of the past. Every human being has been hurt by the actions or words of another person or group, and if you do not practice forgiveness, you might be the one who pays most dearly.

"Nelson Mandela said, 'Resentment is like drinking poison and then waiting for the other person to die.' You will only be hurting yourself by holding on to previous contentions and rancor, while forgiveness can lead you to physical, emotional, and spiritual peace. By deciding to let go of resentment and thoughts of revenge, you will free yourself from the control of any person who may have harmed you.

"Many people say they can forgive," he continued, "but they do not seem to be able to forget. That means that they have no plans to genuinely forgive, and their forgiveness is not complete. When you remember and dwell on the things that you say you have forgiven, you are reliving the past and bringing it forward to the present moment.

"Yacoub, you must also forgive yourself. Do not beat yourself over the head with guilt and regret. If you do, you are emotionally living in the past. You do need to recognize your own former shortcomings; otherwise, you cannot correct your course. But it is detrimental to your success if you keep condemning yourself for past mistakes.

"Forgiveness is actually nothing more than letting go completely," my teacher concluded. "When you forgive, you unconditionally let go of the past. You are then free to be your true self in the here and now."

Wealth, Service, and Life's True Purpose

As our time together that morning waned, Rabbi Avraham voiced a few other relevant things he had on his mind. I listened carefully.

"My friend," he advised while I sipped the last of my coffee, "as you climb up the ladder of success to wealth and abundance, be humble. Do not ever brag about your prosperity; do not talk at length about your accomplishments. Your successes are mainly accomplished as a result of your faith, and true faith is never prideful. Let your unwavering faith shine through in all your transactions and undertakings.

"Let every action you take be the expression and evidence that you are already rich. Words are not necessary to communicate that truth to others, as your actions will speak louder than your words.

"Do not be tempted to seek power over other people. Anyone who desires to intoxicate himself with that kind of power lives a miserable existence.

"In order for you to master your destiny, you must be of service to others. As I have told you, the wealth you accumulate will be in direct proportion to the service you render. You must be a service-oriented leader. The secret of true wealth is being passionate about your purpose and endeavoring to enhance the lives of those around you."

I interrupted my revered teacher to ask, "How did you find your true purpose in life?"

He beamed. "People are always seeking their purpose in life. As far back as the fourth century B.C., Aristotle was pondering life's purpose and developing his theory that everything in life has a purpose.

"It is very simple to find one's purpose in life, Yacoub. Your purpose is what you love doing. It is what gives you a sense of direction and creates meaning for your life. So, what do you love doing? If you had 50 million dollars in your bank account right now, what would be your reason to get out of bed tomorrow morning?"

I immediately replied, "Well, I love listening to you and learning from you. Even if I had 50 million dollars in my bank account, I would still be on time for my next lesson."

Rabbi Avraham laughed heartily. "I am pleased that you plan to maintain your integrity and be on time—even after earning 50 million dollars!"

He then quickly asked, "Well, how about owning a gym?"

I replied, "I love training my clients. I am passionate about helping people transform their physiology. Now, with all the insights you have been sharing with me, I can help them transform their self-image and give meaning to their lives beyond their physical body."

My respected teacher then took a moment to magnify his unique role as my mentor and counselor.

"The day will come," he said earnestly, "when you will share our story and these insights with others. Just remember, my friend, you must be the embodiment of the insights you are sharing. Your way of being must reflect what you are teaching."

5

Meditation and Becoming

A few days later, we met on a humid, slightly overcast morning. As I opened my sliding glass door and stepped out, I saw my teacher sitting at the far side of his balcony. A plastic bag was lying near the railing on my side.

"There is a digital audio voice recorder in the bag," Rabbi Avraham explained. "It is a guided meditation that I made in my own voice for you. Both the recorder and the recording are gifts to you, my friend. I want you to begin meditating today. Do it once a day for twenty minutes this first week. Thereafter, I want you to meditate twice daily."

I expressed gratitude for his kindness and generosity.

"Have you ever meditated before?" he asked.

I was almost embarrassed to answer. "Well, I tried to listen to guided meditation on YouTube a couple of times. The first time my mind was jumping all over the place, and the second time I fell asleep and almost missed my appointment with a client."

The rabbi smiled. "For you to be successful, it is important that you be in a relaxed state. I am sure you will enjoy the journey you are about to embark upon."

I replied, "Rabbi, I'm excited about including meditation in my daily routine. I'll start immediately after our session today."

At that moment, I realized that I had not brought my usual double espresso with me. Coffee can be very addictive, and I wondered if my craving for Rabbi Avraham's teaching had somehow surpassed my craving for coffee.

He firmly instructed me to avoid trying to quiet my mind when I sat for meditation, warning me that if I tried to do so, my thoughts would rise up with ten times their original force. The only way to master the mind, he explained, was through constant practice coupled with determination.

Rabbi Avraham added that meditation should be my inner shelter. It should blossom, unfold, and flower. Whenever I feel overwhelmed with the noise of the outside world, I can move into my shelter.

"Yacoub," my rabbi emphasized, "I want you to sit and listen to the sound of my voice on the recording. Sit comfortably, with your back straight and your eyes closed. Don't just hear with your ears but listen with your emotions. Be in the here and now, and bathe in the awareness of your inner being. By doing so, you will rejuvenate yourself. You will come out of the meditation renewed and primed to face any challenges you are facing. That is the course to true meditation."

As we concluded our discussion on meditation, I felt impressed to express my gratitude for his compassionate guidance. "Rabbi," I said, "I always feel better after our meetings. Your teachings never fail to make me feel elevated, if that makes sense."

He smiled. "It does makes sense, Yacoub. You must always be aware of the influence of those around you, especially as you seek to experience your authentic self. If you associate with the wrong crowd, you might start lowering your expectations of yourself to their level. Therefore, you must carefully choose associates who will elevate your wholesome aspirations."

"I would love to acquire your qualities," I said, hoping that someday this would come to pass.

"Oh, my friend," he replied, "you are already in possession of all these qualities! Once you are awakened, you will realize that they are within you. All you need to do is search inward."

The Inner Path to Becoming

Rabbi Avraham was eager to continue this line of thought. "It is important to understand your needs as a human being," he said. "Such needs continually influence your thoughts, feelings, and behaviors. We all have higher-level needs and lower-level needs.

"The spirit is the main component of a human being. The truth is that we are not ensouled bodies; we are embodied souls. According to Abraham Maslow's hierarchy of needs, a person is always 'becoming' and never remains static.

"Our souls are anxious for continuous growth, expansion, and ultimate transcendence to reach the infinite. While you are growing as a soul, you become aware that you have the need to be of service to others."

I was taking notes feverishly as my teacher was speaking. Seeing my efforts, he slowed down so I could capture every word he was saying. When I finally stopped writing, he continued.

"In addition to satisfying our higher needs for growth and being of service to others, we must also satisfy our own basic needs."

I was curious. "What are those needs, sir?"

"There are four," he said.

"The first need is for physiological or biological necessities, such as food, air, water, shelter, clothing, sleep, etc. If these needs are not fulfilled, our bodies cannot function properly.

"The second need is for physical, emotional, and financial safety and security. People want to experience order, predictability, and control over their lives.

"The third need is for love and belonging as we strive to build healthy interpersonal relationships.

"And the fourth need is for esteem—to feel unique, respected, accepted, and valued by others."

The rabbi inserted a note of caution with respect to the fourth basic need. "It is very important," he insisted, "that you fulfill your own needs without violating the rights of others. You should never satisfy your need to feel unique by bringing other people down and criticizing them. You can fulfill that same need by building them up."

He added a final reminder. "Always remember, Yacoub, that there are positive, empowering ways to fulfill and satisfy your needs as well as disempowering, harmful ways. How you decide to conduct your life means the difference between success and failure."

"Can you give me an example, please?" I pressed.

"Of course. Let us say you value the need for safety and security most. Suddenly, an opportunity comes your way to open your own gym. But with that opportunity comes considerable risk and uncertainty.

"Think about it. Are you going to play it safe by allowing your need for security and safety prevent you from stepping out of your comfort zone and taking hold of that opportunity? Or are you willing to rely upon the sense of safety and security provided by your vibrant new self-image, which leads you to trust that no matter what happens, you will always find a way to thrive?"

I pondered his scenario for a few moments and then said, "I understand."

Rabbi Avraham had the ability to explain things in simple terms, which helped me come to a clear understanding of his teachings. He always stayed on the topic until I had fully embraced what he was saying, and he repeated concepts when he felt that I did not entirely understand.

He then delivered his final message of the day.

"Our book of Proverbs states: 'Wisdom is the principal thing; therefore, get wisdom: and with all thy getting get understanding.' Yacoub, understanding comes through studying and learning. Along the way, understanding will surely turn into faith and then into action, and you will have the wisdom and fortitude to achieve your goals and create the life you love."

Our session was concluded, and I went inside, excited to listen to the guided meditation prepared by my esteemed teacher.

6

The Universal Laws

When the month of June arrived, I experienced mixed emotions. Dade County had approved the reopening of the gym, and I was excited to go back to work. But I was also disheartened that I would not be able to meet with my teacher as often.

Rabbi Avraham had provided a wealth of hope and joy in my time of despair, and I assured him that I would still love to visit with him regularly. So, we agreed to meet on Sundays.

The day before I returned to work, this good man shared with me some of the most important information and counsel I would ever receive. The moment we were settled on the respective corners of our balconies, he got right down to business.

As Real As the Law of Gravity

"Yacoub," he began, "when you understand and apply certain universal laws, achieving your goals will become easy and natural. If you understand them, you will become more self-aware. If you adhere to them, you will work in harmony with the universe and achieve higher levels of consciousness. It is vital that you understand and obey these laws in order to make your life better and become the master of your destiny."

I had never heard of such a thing as universal laws. "Why are they called universal laws?" I asked.

My rabbi explained, "They are universal laws because they are independent of any given culture and are applicable to all humankind. Also, unlike other phenomena in the universe, they are constant, unchangeable, and not subject to personal opinions. They operate whether someone accepts them or not. If we disregard these laws, however, we must pay the price that inevitably follows."

Rabbi Avraham must have seen the confused look on my face because he quickly provided an example. "Yacoub, if you ignored the law of gravity and jumped off your balcony, wouldn't the results be catastrophic?"

I agreed. "Yes, sir, it sure would!"

He leaned forward in his chair. "Well, the universal laws I am speaking of are as real as the law of gravity."

I nodded my acceptance of his statement.

Eager to learn these universal laws, I sat on the edge of my seat, ready to write. Physically taking notes was the best way for me to learn. Writing caused me to think, my thoughts created images in my mind, and those images produced feelings, thus increasing my ability to absorb useful knowledge.

My rabbi recognized his teaching moment and began right away.

The Law of Oneness: Connected to Everything

"The first universal law is the Law of Oneness. It is the law upon which all other universal laws are based. Albert Einstein said, 'Everything is energy. And that's all there is to it.'

"Everything consists of, and exists as, energy. This energy is expressed in different ways. Some call it universal consciousness, some call it nature, and some call it 'ether.' I call it God.

"The energy of which I speak is everywhere at once; it penetrates and permeates all things living or material. Hence, everyone and everything is connected to everyone and everything else in this world. Your thoughts, words, and actions affect others and the whole universe around you.

"The higher your awareness, the more you will experience being connected to everything. It is important for us as a human race to understand this law and realize that our thoughts, feelings, and actions must be for the good of all."

The Law of Cause and Effect: The Law of Karma

I took a deep breath as Rabbi Avraham continued. "The next law I will tell you about is the Law of Cause and Effect."

"Excuse me," I politely interjected. "You have previously mentioned this law. Isn't it the one stating that every action causes an equal reaction?"

He nodded. "Indeed, it is. A positive action will result in a positive reaction and a negative action will result in a negative reaction. I am sure you have heard the saying 'We reap what we sow.' Some people call this law the law of karma, without understanding that *karma* is an ancient Sanskrit word that literally means 'action.'

"The great essayist and poet Ralph Waldo Emerson called the Law of Cause and Effect 'the law of laws.' Everything in the entire universe happens according to this law. There is nothing coincidental. Every effect must have a cause, and every cause must have an effect. Accordingly, we have a continuous, never-ending cycle of cause and effect. It's the domino effect.

"Human beings always have the power to choose. Understanding this law will help you make good choices. Before making any decision, you must always ask yourself, 'What are the effects of this decision?' If the effect will bring goodness to you and those around you, then proceed. If not, then it would be better to reevaluate your choice and make another decision."

The Law of Vibration: Energy and Frequencies

"The next law I will tell you about is the Law of Vibration," my rabbi said. "This law states that everything is energy and everything has its own frequency of vibration.

"You see, your thoughts and feelings have their own vibrations. The higher your level of awareness, the higher your frequency. The higher your frequency, the easier it is for you to attract things, ideas, people, and situations of the same high frequency. You see, vibrations attract similar vibrations. We connect with like-minded people in this universe because they are on the same wavelength as we are."

"So," I ventured, "you and I connected because of the Law of Vibration?"

"Yes," Avraham confirmed. "We connected because we are at the same frequency.

"You can use the Law of Vibration to manifest your desires. All you have to do is match your vibration with that of what you want.

"Albert Einstein said, 'Match the frequency of the reality you want and you cannot help but get that reality. It can be no other way. This is not philosophy. This is physics.'

"That is the reason I previously told you to stop looking at your current circumstances and start looking at the things you want to create in your life. And that is why I want you to stop letting the outside world and other people control your emotions.

"Pleasant emotions are high vibrations, and bitter emotions are low vibrations. You must choose what you think and feel, regardless of your surroundings and life circumstances. Your duty is to guard and fine-tune your vibrations."

"But how can I elevate my vibrations?" I asked.

"By reading, studying, repeating your affirmations, and meditating," he replied without hesitation.

Right then and there, I realized that all the daily rituals my teacher had recommended were for the sole purpose of elevating my vibrations to a higher frequency. He knew they would ultimately bring a world of new possibilities and realities to my life.

The Law of Attraction: Manifesting Success

I knew the rabbi was thoroughly enjoying himself as he continued.

"A complement to the Law of Vibration is the Law of Attraction. Although I did not mention the law by name, I have already taught you its basic concepts.

"This law comes into play when you think of a clearly defined goal such as being the owner of your multimillion-dollar gym. You then use your imagination and the power of visualization to put images of that gym on your vision board and in your mind, and you supplement those images with positive affirmations and act as if you were already the owner of that gym.

"All this will impress those images onto your subconscious mind, causing you to have the same vibration and frequency as the good things you desire. Consequently, you will take an inspired action, which will produce the results you aspire to and cause your goal to materialize.

"In other words, my son, you become what you think about. You can only hold it in your hand after you can see it in your mind. Successful people know that repeating the same thought day after day, with faith and a positive attitude, enables that thought to manifest itself in their lives."

The Law of Inspired Action: From Dream to Reality

Rabbi Avraham was clearly in his element as he pressed on.

"Next is the Law of Inspired Action. As real as all these laws are, they will not have an effect on anything in your life until you engage in physical actions that are in harmony with your thoughts, ideas, goals, and desires. The Law of Inspired Action is required for your thoughts and desires to be realized in the physical world. You must not think something and then act counter to that thought.

"Acting on our ideas and aspirations is almost always the most difficult thing to do. Thinking and talking about something are very different from actually following through with it. When you talk about it, it is only a dream; when you visualize it, it becomes achievable; but when you act upon it, it becomes a reality that cannot be denied.

"While the Law of Attraction is about vibrationally aligning yourself with whatever it is you desire, the Law of Inspired Action is about realizing your goals through acting upon them. Such actions must be inspired and directional but should not be forced and chaotic."

As my teacher was speaking, I was taking careful notes and wondering how many more universal laws there were.

Rabbi Avraham had a highly evolved intuition. I had often felt that he could read my thoughts. He suddenly stopped and said, "My dear friend, I think this is enough for today. There are more universal laws that I will convey to you when we meet next time. For now, if what I have imparted to you makes you think and ponder, then that's a good place to start."

Rabbi Avraham concluded, "Now that you are going back to work, I want you to remember that to achieve and maintain success, it is vitally more important to work harder on yourself than you do on your job. This observation has proven to be true in both my personal and professional life, and it is something I have seen work wonders for many other successful people. I want you to conscientiously continue with your daily rituals."

The universal laws he had taught me all sounded so

simple and yet so profound. I resolved to put them into practice. I had learned so much that day that I could only imagine what our next meeting would bring.

7
More Universal Laws

After the session, I went for a jog on the boardwalk by my Bal Harbour condo. As I was jogging, I contemplated the different laws that Rabbi Avraham so masterfully shared with me. I reflected upon my own life and observed how those laws had been operating in it. When I had volunteered to help my elderly neighbors, I did so in a selfless manner. That altruistic contribution gave me the highest inner joy. The gratitude in my neighbors' eyes rewarded me with the utmost fulfillment. I felt connected with each of them at a profound level. I felt that we were all connected. I felt *oneness*.

I realized that performing these selfless actions had led to my treasured relationship with my teacher. That was the Law of Cause and Effect in full display. When someone puts out good, *good* must come back. Nothing happened by chance or luck; everything happened as a direct result of my actions.

I grasped that life doesn't play favorites. What I attracted into my life was a direct effect of the causes I brought into existence.

Sunday could not come soon enough.

The Law of Perpetual Transmutation of Energy: From Acorn to Mighty Tree

A week had gone by, and I was excited to continue our discussion of universal laws. I was already on my balcony at 6:30 A.M., counting the minutes until our session started. The glimmer in Rabbi Avraham's eye confirmed that he was pleased to see me as well.

Rabbi took his usual seat on the far side of his balcony and regarded me closely. "Yacoub, have you ever seen a mighty oak tree?"

As I nodded, I immediately thought of Arnold Schwarzenegger. His nickname was "the Austrian oak" because of his powerful physique. While I was growing up, he had been my idol, and I often watched his movie *Pumping Iron.*

"Well," my mentor observed, "the acorn is the seed of the mighty oak tree. The tiny acorn seed, in its miniscule shell, holds the potential to become an enormous tree. The same is true of you, Yacoub. You have the potential to grow like that oak tree.

As Rabbi Avraham said that, shivers went down my spine. I desired growth with every cell of my being. My soul was yearning for continuous expansion. I was sitting across from greatness. I knew without a shadow of a doubt that my mentor's teachings were providing me with all the intellectual and spiritual nutrients I needed to grow from a tiny acorn into a giant oak tree with hefty pronged roots, solid trunk, and numerous branches stretching into the heavens.

I leaned in, listening intently.

"The image of the oak tree takes us to the next law," Avraham announced. "It is the Law of Transmutation of Energy, which states that energy moves in and out of physical form. Energy cannot be created or destroyed, but it can be converted from one form to another.

"Your thoughts are creative energy, and they are always moving into physical form. Lao Tzu stated this beautifully: 'Watch your thoughts; they become your words. Watch your words; they become your actions. Watch your actions; they become your habits. Watch your habits; they become your character. Watch your character; it becomes your destiny.'"

As Rabbi Avraham spoke, I recognized anew that the affirmation and visualization rituals I had been diligently performing were for the sole purpose of influencing my thoughts and hence creating my destiny.

"Change is the only constant in life. You must learn to accept it, and you must always strive to change yourself for the better."

The Law of Relativity: Keeping Perspective

My rabbi smiled a little as he introduced the next universal law. "And now," he said, "we will explore the Law of Relativity. This law should be a pendant around your neck in times of hardship.

"The universe will give you challenges, but you have to keep a sense of perspective because there are plenty of people who have harder times than you have. Always be grateful, because everything is relative. And there is more than one perspective in any situation.

"A situation is not necessarily good or bad. You are the

one who assigns meaning to things and events. You can choose either an empowering or a disempowering meaning, and there will always be consequences. As the great German poet-philosopher Johann Wolfgang von Goethe advised his followers, 'Choose wisely; your choice is brief and yet endless.'

"Remember that life is happening *for* you and not *to* you. Everything in our material world is made real only by our relationships or in comparison with other things. Every human being is superior to another human being in one area and inferior to him in another area. Never compare yourself to others. Do not even compete against others. Instead of competing, you must create."

Listening to my teacher's remarks, I remembered that I placed higher in powerlifting competitions when I focused solely on maximizing my strength and perfecting my technique instead of on my fellow competitors.

The Law of Polarity: Seeds of Empowerment

"There is also the Law of Polarity," he continued. "This law states that everything in existence has an equal and exact opposite. In one of the books I gave you, Napoleon Hill said, 'Every adversity, every failure, and every heartache carries with it the seed of an equivalent or greater benefit.'"

I quickly interjected, "Yes, sir, I finished reading *Think and Grow Rich,* and I have started the second book you gave me."

He seemed pleased to hear that. He then proceeded with his explanation of the Law of Polarity.

"You cannot experience success without going through failure. You cannot appreciate joy without having experienced sadness. Everything in life just 'is.' We make it into a negative or a positive by the meaning we give to it.

"Keep in mind that something good can always come out of something negative. Look for the good in people. Use your perception to see both sides of a person or a situation. The late Wayne Dyer said, 'When you change the way you look at things, the things you look at change.' You will be empowered and inspired by how much good you see."

The Law of Rhythm: Life Has Its Tides

Rabbi Avraham asked, "Yacoub, have you observed how many things happen in cycles?"

When I nodded, he continued.

"Well, that is because of the next universal law, which is the Law of Rhythm. Everything has its time. Nothing lasts forever. That goes for people, seasons, and experiences.

"After an unpleasant cycle, there can be a good and successful cycle. In the Torah, Joseph is an example of that truth. He suffered through many hardships, but in the end, he rose to become the most powerful man in Egypt next to Pharaoh.

"If life is tough and challenging, know that it will change. Things happen for a reason, and they happen at the right time. Life has its tides; all things rise and fall. Like a pendulum, whenever something swings to the right, it must then swing to the left.

"Everything is either growing or dying. It's the circle of creation. The key is not to allow negative thoughts to penetrate your consciousness when you are in a downswing but to know that good times are ahead."

The Law of Gender: Feminine and Masculine Energies

After a brief silence, Rabbi Avraham began to speak again. "There is one last law I will share with you," he declared (and I breathed a small sigh of relief). "It is the Law of Gender."

I shot him a puzzled look. "Let me explain," he said.

"This law decrees that everything in nature is both male and female. It has less to do with biological sex than with the notion of masculine and feminine energies. Both are required for life to exist. There must be a balance between these energies.

"The Law of Gender further states that all seeds have maturation periods before they manifest. Likewise, ideas are spiritual seeds and also have maturation periods before they manifest in the physical world. A specific period of time must pass before your ideas are manifested in the physical world, and it is important not to rush the process. Everything will occur as it should."

My teacher concluded his masterful lesson with only a few more words.

"Yacoub," he counseled, "be sure to heed each of these universal laws, and expect great things to happen in due time."

"I will do my best," I promised.

"Good," he said with a warm smile. "My friend, you have been very patient listening to an old man talk about so many mysterious laws. I thank you for that, and I feel certain that you will embrace their value. For now, I bid you adieu. I will look forward to our next meeting."

We waved affectionately across our balconies, and I left to begin my day.

8

Transformation

Although I went back to work after the pandemic lockdown had been ended, I continued to do food shopping for the elderly residents in my building. Giving back tapped into the deepest part of my soul and enabled me to be more like my teacher.

A Spiritual Apprenticeship

The more I became like Rabbi Avraham, the more I felt a shift in my consciousness. I began to perceive my environment in a new way, a way in which I was not separate from the universe and others. I was developing a profound sense of gratitude and appreciation for my life, both present and future, and I was also becoming more compassionate toward others and myself. For the first time, I had started to practice self-love.

In the past, I had enjoyed the attention I received at the gym because of my muscular body and my expertise in the field of fitness. This attention had satisfied my need to be unique and significant. It was all about looking good.

On my first day back at the gym after the lockdown ended, I could not help noticing that my inner self had been undergoing a profound transformation during my time away from work. I was now focused more on my clients' well-being than on their good opinions of me. That was a very liberating experience.

In the beginning, Rabbi Avraham's mentorship had been centered on the science of achievement. As our teacher-student relationship progressed, however, it had evolved into a spiritual apprenticeship. My rabbi was masterful as he embraced both the physical and the spiritual worlds.

The True Purpose of Religion

My personal training business at the gym started to pick up a little, and the younger clients began coming back. Although we were all wearing face masks, the older adults were still hesitant to return to the gym, which was understandable in the circumstances.

One of my returning clients was Elaine, who was in her late thirties. In addition to being attractive and intelligent, she was also quite spiritual. She was into Kabbalah, transcendental meditation, and other spiritual practices.

Before COVID-19 hit the United States, she had regularly attended various spiritual retreats. She told me about one of those retreats in San Ramon, California, at which she would visit an Indian woman, Ammachi, known as the Hugging Saint, whose mission was to spread the message of love throughout the world.

At the time, I wondered how a wealthy and successful businesswoman like Elaine would be interested in that kind of activity. After I met Rabbi Avraham, however, it all made sense to me.

Elaine was on a spiritual journey and considered herself a soul first and foremost. She did not allow her material possessions to be obsessions in her life. She was exceptionally down to earth, treated everyone at the gym with respect, and was always on time for her weekly sessions with me.

The appealing thing about Elaine was that she did not wear her faith on her sleeve. Her spirituality was expressed in the way she conducted her life and treated others around her.

After encountering Elaine and many other persons of different faiths and backgrounds in South Florida, I came to the conviction that the true purpose of religion is to help us rise to the divinity within us.

Partaking of the Gifts

Upon the conclusion of my training session with Elaine one Thursday evening, she said, "Yacoub, I must tell you that I can't help noticing how much you have changed over the past few months. Please don't get me wrong. You are an amazing guy, and you've always been an extraordinary, knowledgeable personal trainer. But now—now you somehow seem more centered, balanced, and at peace."

I smiled and said, "Well, thank you, Elaine. Coming from you, that means a lot." I then briefly told her about Rabbi Avraham and my new daily rituals.

The following Tuesday was my next session with Elaine. We always started with abs and core exercises, followed by working out legs on Tuesdays and upper body on Thursdays. No matter how hard I pushed her, she was always up for the challenge. She had an awesome attitude.

At the end of the session, Elaine thanked me for another great workout. Then she reached into her gym bag and handed me a book as a present. It was entitled *Teachings of Rumi.*

She explained that Rumi was a Muslim Sufi Mystic whose poetic work and teachings are studied and revered throughout the world, including the western hemisphere. With a knowing smile she added, "Rumi's transformation happened when he met his teacher, Shams of Tabriz."

The Highest Form of Friendship

As I continued to perform my daily rituals in accordance with my teacher's guidance, he shared more mystical, spiritual teachings with me. Through these teachings I came to realize that the mysticism of all religions is about human transformation and spiritual connection rather than about dogma or rigid rules. I mentioned to Rabbi Avraham that I would never have come to these realizations if I had not met him.

He replied, "Yacoub, every teacher has his past, and every student has his future. The time will come when the student will become the teacher.

"It is very important to understand the role of a teacher, which is to remove the layers of ignorance obscuring the authentic essence of his student. A teacher will help his student on the journey to self-realization. The teacher-student relationship is the highest form of friendship because it is founded on unconditional love and wisdom.

"The teacher's actions must never be led by his own ego.

In addition, a true teacher should have a good understanding of and experience with the knowledge being taught. His thoughts, words, and actions must coincide with his teachings, and he must radiate compassion and humility."

Moments of Peace and Enlightenment

As time passed and I faithfully observed my daily rituals, each twenty-minute meditation began to feel as if it were a warm and comforting spiritual bath. Both the past and the future disappeared during those quiet times, and I was able to experience what living in the Now really meant. The pendulum of my mind stopped swinging back and forth, and my mind reached a level of stillness I had never known before. I dwelt in that peaceful state through every session.

As the November elections approached, I overheard political conversations of some of the gym members. For me, the conversations were just static noise in the background, and I chose not to pay much attention to them. Some members, who identified themselves as Republicans, were speaking poorly of Democrats, and some Democrats were doing the same thing to Republicans. Being from the Middle East, where people are not allowed to openly voice their opinions, I felt grateful to live in a country where differing opinions could be freely expressed. I only wished those gym members using derogatory language could be introduced to Rabbi Avraham's words: "Start looking for the good in people. Use your perception to see both sides of a person or a situation. You will be empowered and inspired by how much good you will see."

Toward the end of that year, my stillness began to extend

beyond the times when I was meditating. I enjoyed this peace while working out, training my clients, and even driving. I actually stopped getting all worked up by the recklessness of some of our more aggressive South Florida drivers.

I stopped reacting to people and situations, and instead I started responding. As I did that, I felt in control of the outside world and became an intuitive observer of my own thoughts and emotions. I was able to stand back as a witness when certain thoughts and emotions popped up.

Solutions to problems started to appear spontaneously. I felt calmer, more relaxed, and connected with my intuition instead of relying solely on my logical mind. Mine was becoming a more meaningful life with each passing day.

As those internal changes were occurring, my outside world was also evolving. I started attracting new clients who were kind, pragmatic, sensible, and financially successful. Even better, my spirit seemed to be opening up to some wonderful new possibilities.

Elaine was always my last client each Tuesday and Thursday evening, and we started going to a nearby Starbucks after her sessions ended. I relished those heart-to-heart conversations as we sat outside and enjoyed our green herbal tea.

Our trainer-client relationship quickly developed into a valued friendship. It was not a friendship based on selfish motives. I cared for her because of her character, and her words and actions demonstrated that she felt the same way about me.

When I communicated that observation to Rabbi Avraham, he seemed pleased.

"Yacoub," he observed, "this kind of friendship has become

possible because you are both similar in virtue. You must hold tight to such a friendship, and you will be able to guide each other as you continue your journey into self-fulfillment."

His encouragement rang true to my heart.

9
Awakening

On a Sunday early in the new year as we were seated on our respective balconies, Rabbi Avraham informed me that he would be traveling back to New York the following day. He did not tell me how long he was planning to stay there, but he indicated he had an important matter to attend to.

He would be flying out of Fort Lauderdale, and I asked him if I could drive him to the airport. His voice was subdued as he replied, "Thank you, but I have made my arrangements already, and it is better that I stick to them."

"When will you be coming back to Florida?" I asked. "When will I see you again?"

He replied, "It would be lovely if you could come to New York and meet Daniel and Joshua."

I was thrilled at his invitation. "That would be awesome, Rabbi! I can take a week off next month and fly to New York. I would love to visit you there and meet your sons."

"They are really good men. You will like them," he said.

As my teacher was going into his condo, I noticed that

his gait and posture were a bit different. "Rabbi, is everything okay?" I asked with concern.

He turned around and looked at me for what felt like an eternity. It reminded me of the first time his piercing blue eyes had looked in my direction on that early morning, almost exactly a year earlier.

He gave me a fatherly smile and went into his condo without saying a word.

On January 18, 2021, I went for a jog on the boardwalk. Throughout that one-hour jog, thoughts jostled rapidly through my mind.

It is said that when the student is ready, the teacher will appear. I was so happy and grateful that Rabbi Avraham had appeared in my life. It had been only a few days since he left, and I was missing him in a big way. I could not wait to visit him in February, and at the moment New York seemed very far away.

When I got back to my condo, I checked my phone and saw a missed call from a New York number. A new voice message was from Daniel, Rabbi Avraham's elder son.

My mind could not process the enormity of the news I had just heard. I felt disbelief and denial, and everything inside me shouted "No!" as I struggled to come to terms with that heart-crushing new reality.

I could not tolerate the pain. Every cell in my body was protesting against what seemed to be a cruel, unfair, and incomprehensible twist of fate. I fell to the floor and wept like a child.

My dear friend, mentor, and teacher had gone to his eternal home that very morning.

I do not know how long I wept. Time froze as images of

Rabbi Avraham flashed on the screen of my mind, accompanied by snatches of what he had taught me:

"Yacoub, every moment of your life you are making choices. You can always choose the meaning you give to events and the actions you take.

"Life is energy, and energy can never be destroyed. Therefore, life can never be destroyed. It only passes through various evolutions or progressions, and death is simply a transition from one stage to another."

Merely by remembering his words, I felt his presence. Finally, I composed myself and called Daniel back to convey my condolences. He told me the burial would take place within twenty-four hours.

I was on the next flight to New York.

Before the funeral service, Daniel gave me Rabbi Avraham's yarmulke, saying it was his father's wish that I have it. Although it was not required for a non-Jew to wear a yarmulke in a synagogue, I wore it as a sign of utmost respect to my beloved teacher and his family.

I was seated with Daniel and Joshua on the front row. The service began with prayers, after which the cantor read a moving eulogy that epitomized my teacher's spirit. After his remarks, Daniel, Joshua, and other family members and close friends spoke about Avraham.

Daniel asked me if I would like to say a few words, and I agreed. There was so much I wanted to say, but the words wouldn't come. With a tearful voice, all I could say was "I love you," wishing in my heart of hearts that I had said those words to him on the balcony before he flew back to New York. After more prayers, we went into a private room until the funeral procession began.

Rabbi Avraham's funeral service, which had begun at the synagogue, was completed at the cemetery. My teacher was buried in a simple wooden casket.

I chose to stay in New York for the week-long mourning period. During that time, I observed what great men Daniel and Joshua were. They had the same loving, kind, and authentic demeanor as their father, and they treated me like a family member.

After the seven days of sitting shiva ended, Daniel and Joshua drove me to the airport. On the way, they told me how much their father loved me and how he had often spoken of me over the telephone.

Joshua mentioned that their father had known his days were numbered and chose to spend them teaching and guiding me. Upon hearing that, I could not hold back my tears, and they flowed freely down my cheeks.

Daniel had something else to share. "By the way, Yacoub," he said kindly, "it was our father's wish that you have his apartment in Bal Harbour, and he put that in his will. Here are the keys." He pressed a small keychain into my hand.

Daniel's last words to me were, "You are family. We hope you will stay in touch. And if there is anything you need, please do not hesitate to contact either of us."

On the flight back to Florida, I was lost in poignant thoughts and emotions about so many things Rabbi Avraham had taught me. In those tender moments I felt supported and protected by an ocean of love and kindness.

When One Door Closes . . .

I took an Uber home from the airport. I decided to wait to

enter my rabbi's condo until the following morning at 7:00 A.M.—our usual scheduled meeting time.

At the hour I had chosen, I entered Rabbi Avraham's apartment with reverence and respect. The first thing I did was walk across the hallway and through the living room to his sliding glass door. I slid the door open and stepped onto the balcony.

I saw the chair in which Rabbi Avraham had sat to teach me. I immediately sat in the chair and looked toward my own balcony, yearning to see what he had been seeing. I saw myself looking at my old self through his eyes.

As I sat there in his chair, I realized that Rabbi Avraham's teachings had been about much, much more than financial independence. Indeed, he had given me a deeper and more profound intellectual and spiritual understanding of life itself. His teachings had been about self-realization, self-love, and self-mastery.

At that moment, shivers went up and down my spine as I experienced my new, true self. I was still feeling the pain, but all suffering had ceased to exist, and I clearly heard his voice.

"Yacoub, you are no longer the student. You are the teacher now."

Suggested Materials

The following items have been among my favorites as I have pursued knowledge, understanding, and self-realization. These classics will whet your appetite for learning true principles and eventually achieving self-mastery.

May your journey be rewarding and your enjoyment full as you begin the experience of a lifetime.

Books

Covey, Stephen R. *The 7 Habits of Highly Effective People.*
Hill, Napoleon. *Think and Grow Rich.*
Jensen, Michael C. *Putting Integrity into Finance. A Purely Positive Approach.*
Tolle, Eckhart. *The Power of Now.*
Wattles, Wallace. *The Science of Getting Rich.*

Seminars

Proctor, Bob. *Paradigm Shift.*
Robbins, Tony. *Unleash the Power Within.*
Robbins, Tony. *Date with Destiny.*

Sound Recording

Nightingale, Earl. *The Strangest Secret.*

Made in the USA
Las Vegas, NV
19 July 2021

26680011R20059